Domestic Corpse

Domestic Corpse

poems

Paul Martínez Pompa

Chicago | Los Angeles

Published in the United States by Match Factory Editions, 2025

ISBN 978-1-966253-13-6 (hardcover)
ISBN 978-1-966253-12-9 (paperback)
ISBN 978-1-966253-14-3 (ebook)

Library of Congress Control Number: 2025934790

matchfactoryeditions.com

Book layout by RD Morgan

Cover art and design by Gretchen Hasse

Colophon design by Randy Cochran

for Mijo, for Mija

In the second half of the nineteenth century,
the use of cold in the home
became an index of civilization.
—Tom Shachtman

And you may ask yourself,
"How do I work this?"
—Talking Heads

TABLE OF CONTENTS

[Three.]

[Four.]

What

Think of a tree overseeing a process of murder tools,
except nothing actually dies here.

The tree means someone failed to walk away in time.
The tools mean someone climbed,

almost willingly, into a trunk and listened
for the car to start.

Then. There.
That.

[One.]

Look

Somewhere close to a river that divides a body of people from another
body of people, a gathering of men have left a pile of parts. She

will be found and discarded by men in uniforms who learned to look
the other away. This is what keeps me listening at night

while the rest of the house sleeps. Men who gather
with their desires and their chainsaws. Men

who find but look away. And when I look at my daughter
when she doesn't know I'm looking, what blooms

like a chorus of fingers from my chest
and wraps itself around my throat?

No matter how much I wash my hands,
they still smell like hands.

Revolver

She's decided to climb
the small mountain of snow
I've been piling all morning long

beside the garage.
The snow is dirty from alley grit
and is cold against her

unmittened fingers,
but it doesn't matter that it's cold.
Or that there's dirt. What matters

is that there is a mountain
of snow piled beside the garage
and she's decided to climb it.

Language as a Foreign Language

Somewhere is a contract
stating I wed the name breathing
in the next room. Sometimes the name appears
and my name appears and we find ourselves
alone in a hallway, becoming bodies
small enough to pass without touching.

Once upon a time, two bodies disappeared
into a roomful of lust. Each unsure
where its own skin stopped
and the other began. Outside the sun
went on punishing the earth and the moon
couldn't have been more
alive.

Heretic

That side of the window, a falling
snow. This side of the window, a wound
watching a falling snow.

Landscape

Turns out, I looked all wrong. That pretty hill is a process
where routine trees happen. They're obvious

without their leaves but go with a certainty
that can only be called

denial. And those snowy rooftops,
placed just so, conjure a tale of love

gone missing. If you listen carefully
to the trail that leads into town,

you will hear your own killer there,
wanting from a thousand miles away.

Routine

Had we healed in time,
maybe you could look at me
instead of imagining another man
I can't wish away. When we finish,
I take out the trash because it's almost full,
because that's my role, and I'm not coming back
until the lawn is cut. Tell me, who else
could edge a sidewalk so perfectly?
Soon, the land will return to chaos,
and again I will silence it. For you,
I will get on my knees, pull
each weed and come in wanting
only soap and water. Remember
when we used to screw each other,
and mean it?

Three Movements

I'll spend tomorrow on my knees
pleading into the bathtub and halfway through
the vomit and bile, I'll decide
I've had it with this routine
but none of that matters tonight.

•

Someone was shot yesterday
in the liquor store parking lot
next to our homes. Neighbors trade details
in the alley but don't get further than
someone was shot yesterday
in the liquor store parking lot
next to our homes.

•

The cold comes on like an epiphany.
I wrap her in blankets
and we stroller home from the park.
I imagine a fragmented man in the future
granted one wish to return to.
This is it.

Cast Iron Skillet

If you grab the cast iron skillet that's been baking in the oven for an hour, you can pull away as soon as the fire hits your brain, or hold on and let it burn all the way through to your bones. If you pour the gasoline can over the children's naked bodies and light a match, they can try to flee their own skin, or seek refuge in your arms only to find an empty room where your face used to be. Once the flames go out, and the quiet grabs your skull, it won't be the charred bathtub. It won't be the stench. It will be the rise & fall of their tummies that finally get you. Years later, in the middle of night, a car will dart across the window, and you'll never know who. You'll just go on wishing like some damned fool.

Beelzebub, My Beelzebub

got loose in the house
and done made a monster of everything
I touch. Still, the floors stay
spotless. The Christmas tree squeals
with delight. The bellies are full
but the children go longing between
benzo rugs, bourbon doors.
I come-to half-naked on the bed
with a man whose hands I paid for.
The part of the story where she walks out
and just above my head, the birds
sing their denial:
someone.
someone.
someone come and save us.

Thewordlove

I used thewordlove when what I meant was an institution once gave me a prize for orchestrating the best lie out of a slush pile of lies. I traveled the country saying poetry until I didn't mean poetry anymore. These days, I'm more person than poet, but when my baby points to things, I still say their names: *dog. rock. airplane.* Then I realize I'm just screwing up her head.

New Suit with Tags Still Attached

I stand alone
at the front of the funeral parlor
looking down at my dead
grandfather.

[…]

I stand alone
at the back of the funeral parlor
looking up at my dead
grandfather.

Papacito

Not a newborn son I hold in my arms but time
it goes slipping right through
my fingers.

Trope Numero Uno, Uno as in Mexican, Mexican as in *Please Don't Get Yourself Killed, Mijo*

In ten years, you might be seen as a threat.
Your skin one hue too suspicious
for what the unconscious deems
safe enough to keep a gun holstered.

For now, your face is an abundance of light
sent to resurrect the corpses
buried inside my chest.
Your eyes are two wishes
drawing me home and dropping me
to my knees at the doorway.

When you were born, your heart rate plummeted
and you almost died before I could
hold you. The NICU team rushed in
to pummel your body back to life
and into my weeping arms.

I was 14 the first time I was held
at gunpoint. That night, an officer,
maybe a father too, clung to his pistol
the way he might cling to his own child
slipping away. Somehow, he missed
what I'd buried inside my chest
and set me free with just a warning.

Dear officer,
my son can write his own name now
and almost reach the first branch

of the tall tree at school. He waits
for his sister so they can eat ice cream together.
He sits beside me on the floor
and asks if I'm sad when it's actually death he sees
in my face. You can leave your pistol holstered
if you encounter my son in the future.
I promise he is sweet and he is safe.

But I am not.
Please don't get yourself killed,
officer.

Nearness

Such nearness pressed my body with a severity
of music, and among the hydrangeas, who shifted
with each footstep, it was hard to be good.
For a moment, I'd have slept anywhere
on your floor, but an uprising of corpses
lifted my darkness and gave it back
to the sky. How else does one make it
through their body? Through ghosts
pursuing them across oceans and sleepless
rivers. The best lie begins under the vastness
of a bedroom ceiling and collapses
over a trickling sink—its potential for stillness
settles like a mallet inside the chest.

[Two.]

Warm-up Act

We didn't realize the band had already begun to play, so we didn't know what to do with our hands. A rodent worked its way about the crowd's pockets, and I longed for somebody to hug. Not an actual body but a dew-fresh darkness. Besides, if you don't spend quality time wondering who's coming to kill you, what kind of life have you really led?

Family Tree

Ever since I was a child, I've had a problem with authority. So when the shampoo bottle proclaimed it was *as gentle to eyes as pure water*, I took it as an affront not just to me but to my entire lineage, and I did as any self-respecting cowboy would do and emptied the whole thing directly into my eyes. As I stood there naked in the bathtub, longing for disaster, I wondered if this was what Karl really meant by self-abolishing theory. Then it occurred to me, clear as day, that the state collapses primarily as a courtesy, and disaster had been there for me all along. Suddenly, the sycamores made sense, and the sky was less frightening, and I experienced a fleeting sorrow for the solitary officer sent to patrol a long, dark road on a long, dark night. It was a teaching and a forgiving, and I was ashamed, and I was thankful for the lesson in waiting. I hugged the man bathing beside me and told him I'd see him next time which was a lie but the proper etiquette for such an occasion.

Self-portrait as Some Fleeting Self

I already know how this episode unfolds, but I lay in bed fully expecting an intervention to shake me into what I don't want to see and what I do want to see, you see, that monster flung over the chair might actually be an empty coat, but when I flick on the light, it turns out to be a monster after all, thank God.

Upward Mobility

I can hire now a pair of semi-skilled laborers to remove the old cancer from the walls and replace it with a more efficient cancer to keep the children warm through winter. Meanwhile, on the other side of town, a particular woman can't be with a particular man, and a particular man can't be, so the woman moves on to wed another fella, and the man moves on to rake leaves, sticks, whatever dead thing falls from the sky.

Poetry Machine

Then I went behind the garage to murder the rabbit I'd caught in the
Havahart trap. The next day when my party guests asked *what's that stain
on the concrete*, I told them I'd spilled something, and, hey, what do you think
of those hydrangeas I planted over there by the fence?

Madman

It would be nice if a madman kicked down the back door. Then it occurs to me that I am barefoot and at a tactical disadvantage. I set my coffee back on the kitchen table, which isn't just the kitchen table but also the concealment I'll use if a madman kicks down the back door.

The Misfits vs. The Clash

Last weekend, I invited an acquaintance to my asshole with the intention of buttfucking. We were introduced by a mutual friend and had spent several months engaging in occasional, polite texting, which gradually evolved into more frequent, charged banter. We agreed on a time, and he arrived promptly at the doorstep of my asshole, but before entering, he stopped dead in his tracks and said *oh, my goodness, your asshole is beautiful*. I guess I was flattered at first, but as the thrusting ensued, I grew angry. I tried to blow it off and enjoy the buttfucking, but I couldn't get past the presumptuousness of this man who, for whatever reason, assumed that I would have an unkempt hole. He could conceive of beauty, and he could conceive of my hole, but it shocked him that the two could pair together. I felt like a rag. After a couple hours of buttfucking, accompanied by cheese and crackers, my hole was raw, and my acquaintance had work in the morning, so we called it a night. I walked him to the door and thanked him for his visit, but what really went through my head, in a manner of certainty like no other, was not only that the Misfits were a far superior band to the Clash, but also that my acquaintance would never again be invited to the doorstep of my asshole.

English 101

On the first day of Intro to Poetry, I ask students to share their reasons for taking the class. Inevitably, some admit they signed up only because it fulfilled a credit obligation or because nothing else fit their schedules on Mondays and Wednesdays at 11:00AM. They tell me this sheepishly, sometimes with a wave of shame crossing their faces, as if they just confessed to shitting on my beloved's head. What they don't understand is that their indifference to poetry is nothing compared to my heartfelt disdain for it. In fact, I would rank poets just slightly above people who chuck a crying baby against the wall. But that might be too high a rank, because if you asked my mother why she chucked her baby, you'd get a far more honest answer than if you asked a poet why they wrote their poetry.

That Prozac

Suddenly, a gunman appears in the middle of a fashion statement and triggers more meaning than the poet he just exposed. Readers cling to their trauma. A safer narrative is put forth. The body stays in the house, but the head left years ago.

The The

The banks already knew and were called in to explain to the people what they really were. Suddenly, the rodents went scattering like people, and the people went begging like stomachs, and the children, o the children, stood trembling at the door as if there were an inside.

The tanks already knew and were called in to explain to the people what they really were not. Suddenly, the rodents went scattering like people and the people went begging like stomachs, and the children, o the children, stood trembling at the door as if there were an outside.

Testicular

I've never considered the testicles particularly appetizing, and while I wouldn't deem them an outright monstrosity, testicles wouldn't come to mind if I were asked to imagine something beautiful, like springtime cherry blossoms or that vocal thing Clare Torry does on *Dark Side of the Moon*. This was the mindset I tried to inhabit when I found a tiny lump near my left testicle. I was terrified, but if it turned out cancerous, I reasoned, an orchiectomy could be a triumph over tyranny. After all, I could get along fine with one testicle and one penis or, better yet, with one penis alone. Years ago, mother told me that my disposition disqualified me from being authentically gay, for an authentic gay would hold the testicles in the same high esteem as the penis. But what I find far more deplorable than testicles themselves are male writers who write about testicles without even a hint of shame. I swore I'd never write about testicles, and here I am, writing about the cultural logic of late capitalism.

Dead Babies & Other Longings

Today on the 77 bus, from Sayre all the way to Kimball, there was a screaming baby. It was a screaming like you've never heard. The baby's agony became a communal thing, so that the sitters and the standees and even the driver became one united can of misery rolling eastbound into the rising sun. Then I realized that one day, maybe even soon, the baby would be dead. The riders and the driver would be dead too. Some of them would have sincere criers at their funerals. Others would have guests shuffle past their caskets, saying things like "how unfortunate" or "she's in a better place now." I hope at my death there will be complete nothingness, except for maybe that vocal thing Clare Torry does on *Dark Side of the Moon*.

Valentine's Day

Speaking of displaced homelands, how 'bout them short-stroke, gas-operated, 8.38-pound Sig Sauers? Name that goon. They're coming to break your ancestry one hospital bed at a time.

Speaking of trauma bonds, how 'bout them infinitely expanding black holes? In a corner of a room, the empty chair gives nothing & takes nothing. My dearest friends fled their heads anyway, leaving me to walk this high alone. One pharmacy at a time, the peep hole cultivates the most sincere profundity.

Speaking of unlubricated anal play, how 'bout them self-immolating Chicago White Sox? I keep falling in and out of love with shiny meat hooks. The children have been conditioned to adore crumbling institutions as if there weren't cleaner hands to plunder the community. Today, I looked directly through the skyboxes and into the sun. Turns out, there's no such thing as America.

Doormat

The heart yet another collapsing economy, I'd had it with my ghosts and decided to haunt them back. What use is medicine in this romance between the neck and what's sent to snap it? So I held them. I held them and held them until they fell asleep. Every rancid corpse. Each one more adorable than the last.

[Three.]

The Missing Song
for Roberto Harrison

By children I mean walls once imagined
as shelter from the land and its abundance
of militaries. By love I mean rifles
zeroed into their own abandonment
fetish. By skin I mean gravel
piled into piles of broken-colored boys
washing ashore in the thin of night.
By language I mean imposter wounds
draped across my children's
longing. By Roberto I mean bicycle for seeing
water and building a bridge between
disoriented trees. By song I mean soil
smuggled into prison to comfort the aching
flowers. By sobriety I mean a room of corpses,
each one confessing the same empty
river. By giving [up] I mean giving [into]
your makeshift Jesus or whatever burning boat
carries you from one dark town to the next.

More & More the Body Itself a Hoax

[the shank or the icepick]
[the waistband or the front pocket]
[the carotid artery or the brain stem]
[the nylon rope or the extension cord]
[the sawzall or the hacksaw]
[the backdoor or the backseat]
[the deep of the woods or the side of the bridge]

[...   ]

the zip
ties the rubber
gloves the bleach
jugs the duct
tapes the trash
bags the story
resurfaced
rearranged
reconditioned
refashioned
rehearsed
rehoused
reclaimed
repented
restocked

[...   ]

a willing town
to hold your pain / your pain

to furnace the room / the room
to untie their faces / their faces
to subsidize your loss / your loss
to stir the corpse / the corpse
to corpse the corpse / the corpse
the corpse / the corpse

Landscape

The cold is coming and the trees are preparing
as they would for some great death to arrive,
to spill out across the fields, to smother
the earth with sleep beyond any other
promise.

•

Is it criminal for grown men
to ask their dying fathers to pray for them?
For fathers to ask the same
of their dead sons?

•

One by one, each bullet
eased into the magazine, and the light
from the bedroom window,
hardly a trickle now.

Someone / Else

Someone has to aim a flashlight at the face and search an abandoned pair of eyes. Someone has to sift through the overgrown grasses in the vacant lot. Someone has to pile someone else's intestines onto the chest before it can all get bagged and carried away. Someone has to flush the pavement and load the hose back onto the truck. Someone has to knock on a door and wait in the thick night. Someone has to do that too, that job.

Weeping

Sometimes a lifelong weeping
is called for.
Other times a simple tear
hitting the floor
will do.

The Villagers

They took to the streets by the thousands, not knowing
what they were, only that they had been fooled
by the looping flowers overhead, by the faces backing up
from the sewers and murmuring from their bathroom
mirrors, by the beautiful shovels ushered in
to conceal entire continents. One by one
they looked back, each afraid to hear their own
name. And in this arrives a moment for seeing.
When the rifles discover who will submit
and who will blossom. When the heart discovers
what the head's been doing all along.
When the weight of breathing collapses
markets, sending a tremor across the land.
Once upon a time there was a brick,
but there wasn't a hand willing to throw it.

Blindfold

They gave of themselves petal by petal
until no petals were left, or the smell
of so many flowers was reassuring as vermin
continued to feast on dead skin cells.
I could tell you my dreams are full
of bread, but they're not. And how much less
would the burden of proof be
for emptiness? A folded dress? This drawer
wiped cleaned of digital tokens?
I love you from here, a chronic shadow
coupled with looping hysteria.
If only I had a better yard sign,
I could change the world.

In Celebration of Tall, Tall Buildings with Easily Accessible Rooftops, Overlooking the Sidewalk Below

If we look beyond the mess opened up on the concrete,
beyond the shrill of passersby & sirens,

we see confirmation. A promise fulfilled.
Not a tragedy but a mathematics,

predictable & lasting & evermore soothing
than any shoulder to cry on might be.

A Happening, a Not Happening, or

a likelihood frames a man standing over a dead child
or mother

or paradigm he knows as a bedroom
surrounded by trees. Off screen, fear piles

like only refugees do. Each movement
I mistake as my own body floating away,

not how decomposed the corpse appears
but how sudden.

One arm digs while the other
looks on, disbelieving. By ideology, I mean

just how
the dog gets walked around the block.

By windows, I mean windows
opening to brick

walls that help everyone sleep
less soundly. From this distance,

the children look
untouched and the rifles are poised to respond

to something dangerous or something painful
like a community.

Stockpile

What there was of the cold has moved on,
as all spells do, despite a longing for better

illness. With weapons too familiar to mend
the monsters tucked inside, they caught me

staring out the window, suffering against sky
I was no match for. They promised their cancer

was realer than any I could imagine.
And just below my face, a child wandered,

motherless about the floor
through the long and slippery night.

The War on Sleep

Our throats turned out to be so very throat-like.
Open not just to the cold but to the wolves, the apparitions
gathering on the edge of town, the shapeshifters
who began perfecting murder long before the mouths,
too fearful to sleep, began perfecting the sentence,
that make-believe shelter revealing itself
as an unwalkable distance between you
and her hair. Her language, her currency
the most promising betrayal.

•

There was a small boy with a vast crucifix
hanging on his bedroom wall.
I wasn't told its significance
so I made up my own music.
I didn't use the word God
but that didn't mean it wasn't
a begging song.

•

Some nights the shame was hardly noticeable.
Some nights it lay like a corpse across my throat.

•

There was a small man with a vast ocean
happening in his chest.
I inched into night, foolish enough to believe

I might conceal it, hold it in my own
two hands and guide it toward a landfall
dotted with trees, unfeeling any need
to argue their point to passersby.

•

One day, I will go a day without remembering you.
Today, the trees hang like murder
over this never ending town.

Approximations & Other Misaligned Identities

You never knew if you'd be eaten by a bear or tossed headfirst into the darkness of the forest by figures wearing gloves where their mouths should be. You never knew where to run once her face slid through the blinds and into your sleep, which arrived from time to time between mornings revealing themselves as ancestors. You never knew the right moment to enter the conversation that began long before your body and spread itself across your skin in a currency foreign to your birth. You never knew when there'd be a knock at the door and a river asking not for you but for someone with the same name.

Apparition

As if I could mend the mountains, the lakes, the baby trees.
As if I could mend the doorway your breath enters

and exits. It's easier to die than feel
the magnitude of probability. Maybe it's the wind

drifting like mouths to obscure some darker cold
sure to come. I wander into another daybreak

and return having so much and so little to tell.
Apparently, the sun. Apparently, the moon. Apparently,

the sincerest of faces happening on children
until their land is shoveled from beneath their torsos

and replaced with a longing for plastic bags.
Of weaponry. Of personality disorders. Of pharmacies

hustling the latest cave. Soon we saw wolves
and knew only the softest hearts

would make it through winter.

[Four.]

Lit

Like waterlogged children draped
across sharpened landscapes like carved bodies
stitched together by longing like dollar bills
leading to taller piles of filth like hands
reaching beneath abandoned
tarps like stories never meant
to be exhumed, we walk in the darkest
of nights and walk out
a blooming ocean.

Ultimatums

The pines as usual and the homes nothing
like sky, which was a catastrophe
held over our heads. The people took back the town
only to lose it again. Just as it ought to be, a mandate
and a strategy for going awry. There,
among the grocery aisles, I saw a woman
who was your hair and face but someone else's winter
coat, a re-arranging of the lands I fled.
The moment the handle breaks off
the suitcase and everyone inside drowns, or
I loved you like I'd never been abandoned before,
I mean, I've got the heart, but I don't got the talent.

Improvisational Corpse

Our bodies arrive already sliced
into zeros and ones and speech itself
rivers toward loss.
If there were a name for this
it might sound like an empty chair or a hand
squeezing yours one last time
before our mouths part and night swallows
everything.

We know this city will end
but wander on as if there were a way around
each other's darkness. The bedroom a rehearsal
for letting go. The moon the distance between
my head and my heart.

We wake to our children's bodies, reduced now
to a breathing.

It piles like fire under night.

Dead End Mouth

I never knew what I was
saying, I said, Amerika, like a carcass

unearthed from motel bed sheets,
I said sky, like eyes dripping over

a fleeting lover, I said night, like a name
stitched to the scalp along dark stretches

of interstate, I said music, like a softening floor
for sleeping our sickness away, I said shame,

like mother who gifts a bagful of cancer,
her way of saying *I love you, child,*

and she means it
as best she can.

My Father. The Trees. He is Sitting There.

All around my father are trees.
He is sitting in a chair. There is sun

on his face and he is content to sit without
naming the trees nor the chair

nor the sun on his face. He could sit
like this all day if he wanted.

Not naming anything. Dying
without dying anything.

Dome. Stick. Corpse.

Some tuck their dead within
elaborate vaults, or walk it
into the deep of woods and tie it to a tree
so it can't follow them home.

Others let their dead
rot on the floor, the bed,
the kitchen table, unsure
how to discard it
without damaging the children.

How can I suffer consciously
with such beautiful wounds in bloom?
My son who mistakes my face
for anger.
My daughter who mistakes my face
for my face.

Once, there was purpose in the glass
thrown against the wall.
Now, only the sound of light
switched off in separate rooms.

If only I could cut the night
into smaller pieces, I might
swallow it, just barely
choking on the arms and legs,
the hands and feet.

The Moon & All Its Bruises

I asked [for] this bare wall that hits back like an open field
just out of reach of the body's longing to flee.

I asked [for] this floor blessed with a cancer
set to liberate each and every roofline.

I asked [for] this sleep unfolding a heart-felt violence
no town of corpses could ever fulfill.

I asked [for] this moon hung heavy in the night sky
with no ladder, no rope, no Jesus to rise into it.

Retrograde

The way the lamplight
attaches itself to the wall,
revealing just how
humbled the room, the chair,
the emptied sweater
draped over. Time piles.
Habitual faces appear
then carry through the window
into withdrawing
sky. I remember being born.
It was a wantless day, and the trees
flickered with mouths.
And when you came to town
years later, the night rose
in submission.

Coastline

I arrive at a coastline and discover nothing's there either. I sing happy birthday, dear Laura, with a pocketful of surrogate bullets. I drink until I remember everybody's name then go home to watch them sleep. I lie and say I was born into my family's family. I erect a snowman on the front lawn to assure neighbors the devil is real. I decide to make blood in the basement then decide I can't find my hammer. I unplug the music to better hear the neighborhood dogs' unfulfilled longing. I ward off sentences with a guitar my dead grandfather dug out of the garbage. I yield to a neighborhood etiquette that has disappeared entire nation states. I surrender my children into the loving arms of data gathering agencies. I wave hello and happy funeral to my mother, the leaking cup on the floor, my mother, what did they do to my mother?

Soliloquy

Do we really need the ability to speak?
What more is there to say than "yes,"
"thank you,"
"how beautiful this blade
of grass"?

Lunar

The moon is a hammer again,
I mean the moon's gone
happy and there was no exchange,
no reciprocal slipping away. Just ghosts
grabbing at my shoulders for days
until I sat with them, reaching
toward their mouths, into some great nothingness
scarcely more than a distant and fictitious guarantee.
What I remember most was how afraid I was
to see you. Then how pleased. Then how awful
the holiday decor burned up and down
the streets after you left town.
There's an art to this kind of losing
that unfolds something like a towel
under the chin and hands
guiding a spoon toward my mouth.
Each blanket recast as a giving mirror.
Each sky recast as a soothing funeral
that holds song and space for any bruise
willing to look up.

I Told the Tree

I am hurting
and the tree countered:
I am hurting too, see
how my arms grasp at God
all day and fall hollow
all night? The sun rises
only to vow the full magnitude
of my smallness.

The more I looked at the tree,
the more I drowned in others'
injured rivers and their shame
became my sentencing and their wounds
became my binding
and the moon grew distant
and the stars became one
impenetrable cloak
thwarting my way
home.

I Told the Tree

I am healing
and the tree answered:
I am healing with you, see
how the earth lifts us Godward
for the sun to hold our wounds
in its pulsing hands?
All day the sky praises
our children and at night
the moon soothes our ancestors
back to sleep.

The more I looked at the tree,
the more I drank from others'
blooming rivers and their music
became my breathing and their light
became my seeing
and the moon drew closer
and the stars became one
infinite mother
calling my name
home.

Acknowledgements

Grateful acknowledgement is made to the following journals, magazines and anthologies where some of these poems first appeared, sometimes in earlier versions: *TriQuarterly* ("Landscape 1"); *Forklift* ("Dead Babies & Other Longings"); *Make Magazine* ("Look"); *Mandorla* ("Language as a Foreign Language"); *Resist Much/Obey Little: Inaugural Poems to the Resistance* ("The Villagers"); *Spoon River Poetry Review* ("Poetry Machine", "Madman", "Warm-up Act", "Ultimatums", "Approximations & Other Misaligned Identities"). Thanks to the Illinois Arts Council for a monetary prize provided during the early stages of writing this book. Many thanks and much love and peace to the following individuals for their feedback and/or for their support: Yasmine Alamad, Jennie Berner, Daniel Borzutzky, Manjinder Brar, Brenda Cárdenas, Ricky Castro, Nick Demske, Nico Garcia, Steve Halle, Roberto Harrison, Dubravka Juraga, RD Morgan, Justin Petropoulos, Dawn Tefft and Snežana Žabić. Extra special thanks, appreciation and respect to Snežana Žabić and RD Morgan for believing in this book and bringing it into fruition. Lastly, thank you to Johnnie Harris-Pompa, who is and who will always be the light

About the Author

Paul Martínez Pompa (he/him) is a papa, poet and professor who earned degrees from The University of Chicago (B.A.) and Indiana University (M.F.A). His chapbook, *Pepper Spray*, was published by Momotombo Press, and his first full-length collection, *My Kill Adore Him* (University of Notre Dame Press), was selected for the Andres Montoya Poetry Prize. His poetry has earned an Illinois Arts Council Literary Award and has been widely anthologized, including in *What Saves Us: Poems of Empathy and Outrage in the Trump Era*, and *The Breakbeat Poets: New American Poetry in the Age of Hip-Hop*. Chicago Public Radio commissioned his poetry for a project called "In Verse," which aimed to explore the emotional weight of gun violence. He is currently on the editorial board at *Packingtown Review*, a journal of literature and the arts.

www.ingramcontent.com/pod-product-compliance
Lightning Source LLC
Chambersburg PA
CBHW051330120626
46547CB00016B/2471